The Case of the
Missing Caterpillar
A First Look at the Life Cycle of a Butterfly

by Sam Godwin   **illustrated by Simone Abel**

Thanks to our reading adviser:

Susan Kesselring, M.A., Literacy Educator
Rosemount-Apple Valley-Eagan (Minnesota) School District

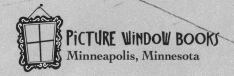

PICTURE WINDOW BOOKS
Minneapolis, Minnesota

First American edition published in 2005 by
Picture Window Books
5115 Excelsior Boulevard
Suite 232
Minneapolis, MN 55416
877-845-8392
www.picturewindowbooks.com

First published in Great Britain in 1999 by Macdonald Young Books,
an imprint of Wayland Publishers Ltd.
Published in 2001 by Hodder Wayland
Hodder Children's Books
A division of Hodder Headline Limited
338 Euston Road
London NW1 3BH

Printed in the United States of America.

Library of Congress Cataloging-in-Publication Data
Godwin, Sam.
The case of the missing caterpillar : a first look at the life cycle
of a butterfly / by Sam Godwin ; illustrated by Simone Abel.
p. cm.—(First look : science)
ISBN 1-4048-0655-5 (hardcover)
1. Butterflies—Life cycles—Juvenile literature. I. Abel, Simone, ill.
II. Title. III. Series.
QL544.2.G64 2005
595.78'139—dc22   2004007315

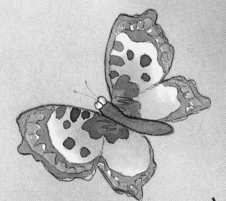

For Yan – SG
For Joyce and Peter with love – SA

What kind of eggs are they?

It is springtime. There is a cluster of eggs

4

hidden under a leaf.

I don't know, but they've been there for about 10 days.

5

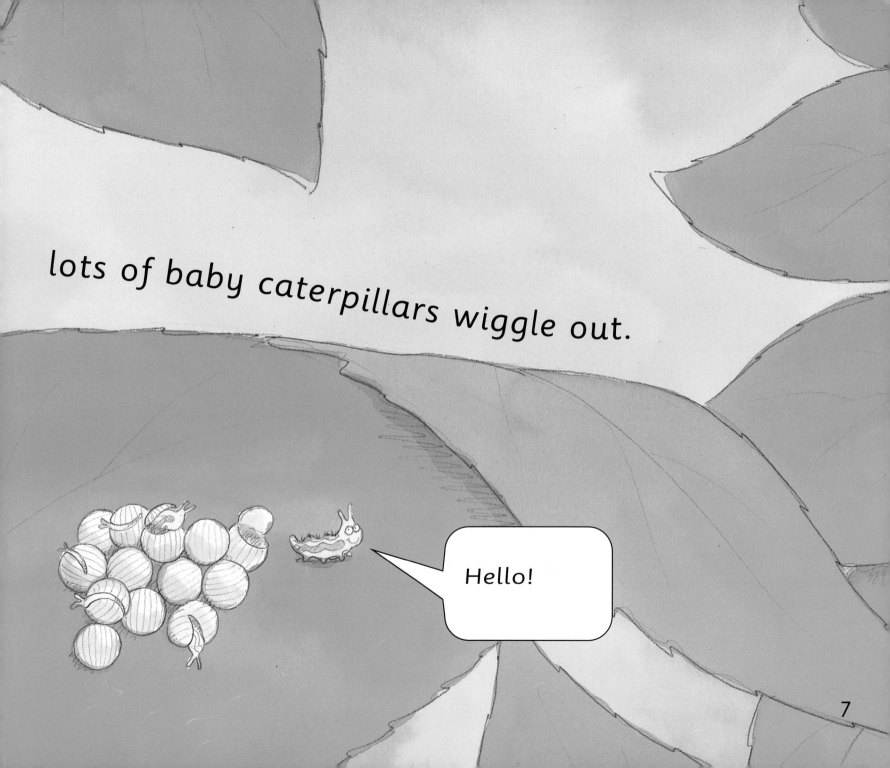

lots of baby caterpillars wiggle out.

Hello!

7

The caterpillars follow each other to the top of the plant.

The nest will protect the caterpillars from bad weather and hungry birds.

They all make a silk nest to hide in.

The caterpillar is very hungry. It munches leaves

If that caterpillar eats any more leaves it will pop!

10

and grows bigger and bigger.

11

That will keep on happening, you know.

it grows too big for its own skin!

13

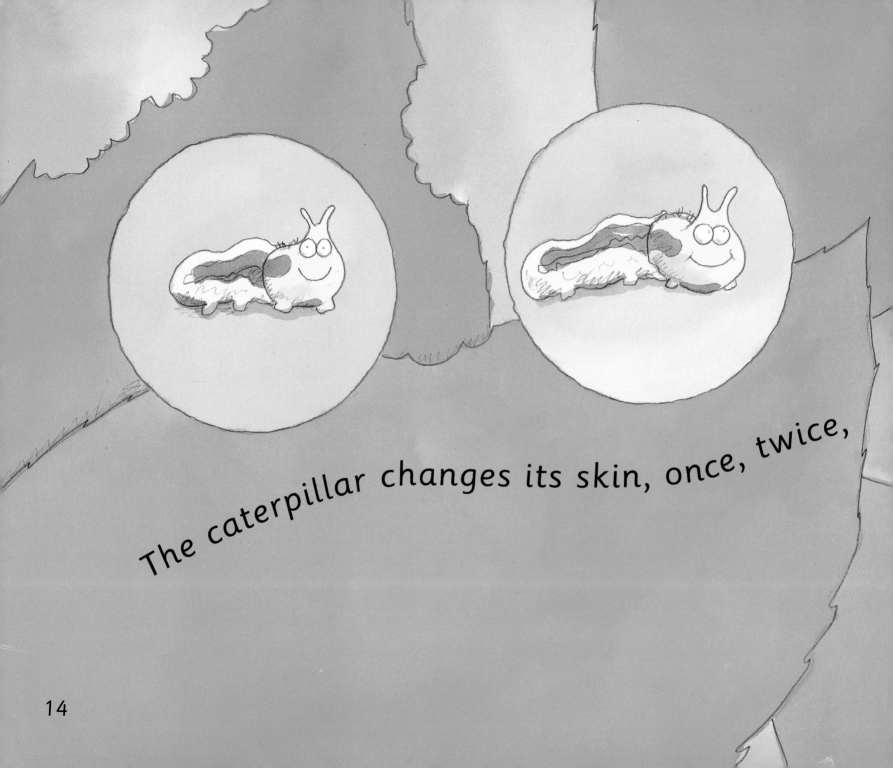

The caterpillar changes its skin, once, twice,

curls up in a leaf.

The caterpillar is hidden
inside a pod.

What's that
up there?

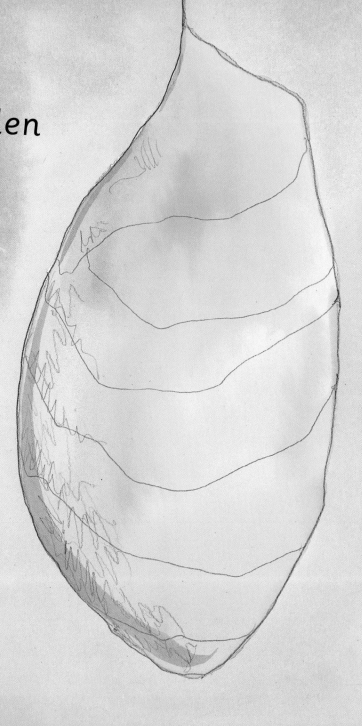

19

For awhile, all is quiet. Then, quite suddenly,

How long does it take for the chrysalis to open?

It depends on what kind of butterfly it is. Some open after only two weeks. Some can stay closed for two years. This one has taken …

the chrysalis begins to split open ...

FOURTEEN DAYS!

21

and a beautiful butterfly climbs out!

23

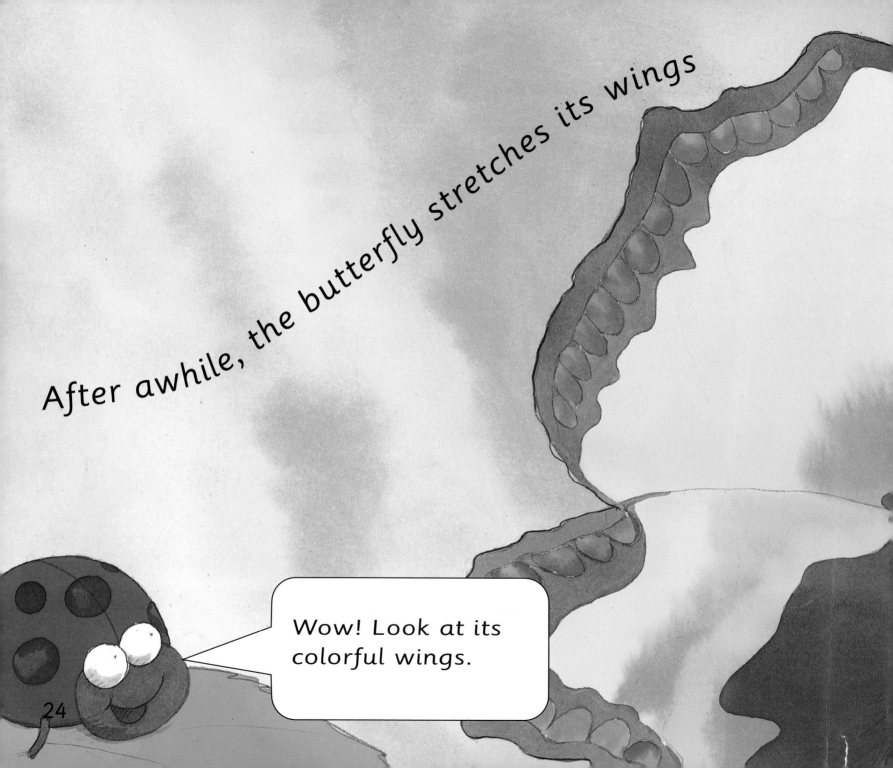

After awhile, the butterfly stretches its wings

Wow! Look at its colorful wings.

24

Four weeks later, the grown-up butterflies lay

I can't wait for these eggs to hatch.

more eggs. The adventure begins all over again.

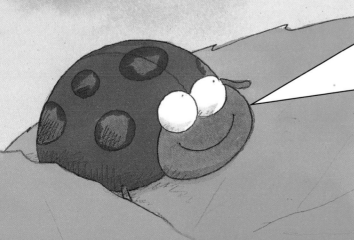

Yes, but this time we'll know where the missing caterpillar is!

27

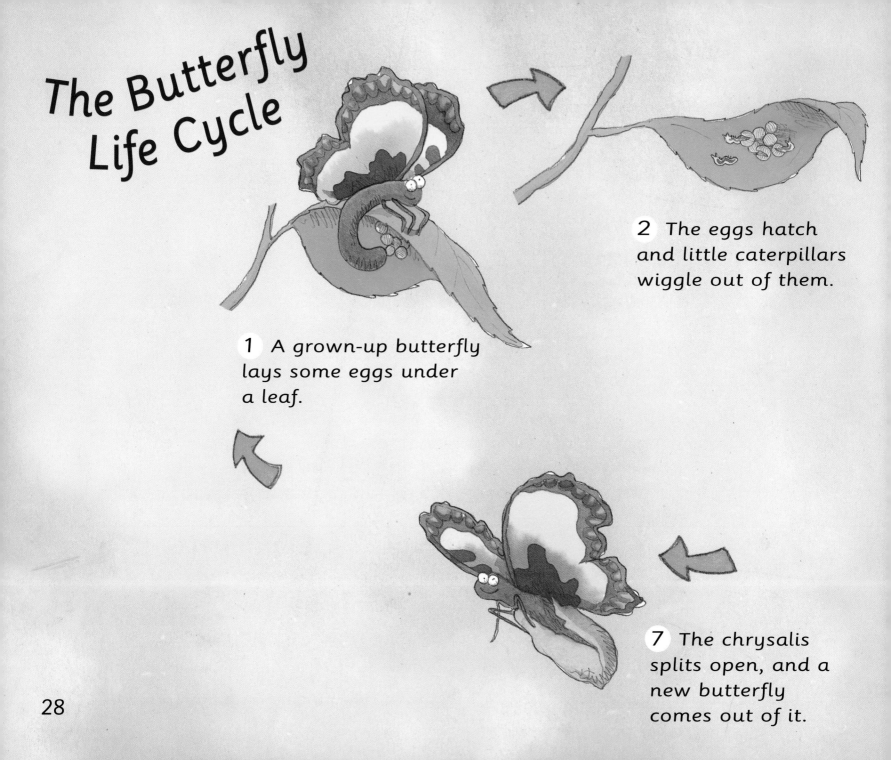

The Butterfly Life Cycle

2 The eggs hatch and little caterpillars wiggle out of them.

1 A grown-up butterfly lays some eggs under a leaf.

7 The chrysalis splits open, and a new butterfly comes out of it.

28

3 The caterpillars make a silk nest on top of a bush. They spend all their time nibbling on leaves.

4 The caterpillars shed their skin.

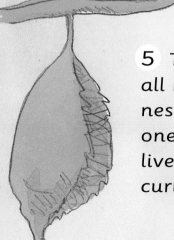

5 The caterpillars all move out of the nest. From now on, one caterpillar will live alone in a curled-up leaf.

6 The caterpillar is inside the chrysalis.

Useful Words

Chrysalis
The pod or case inside which a caterpillar changes into a butterfly.

Hatch
To come out of an egg.

Nest
The home of insects, birds, or animals. Some creatures are born in the nest.

Pod
A kind of shell or case, like a chrysalis.

Fun Facts

- Caterpillars don't have any bones. Instead, they have more than 1,000 muscles.

- Caterpillars get most of their body color from they food they eat. Most caterpillars are green or brown because they eat leaves.

- Butterflies can't fly if their body temperature falls below 86 degrees Fahrenheit (30 degrees Celsius).

- Butterflies can lay up to 500 eggs.

To Learn More

At the Library

Heiligman, Deborah. *From Caterpillar to Butterfly.* New York: HarperCollins, 1996.

Trumbauer, Lisa. *The Life Cycle of a Butterfly.* Mankato, Minn.: Pebble Books, 2002

Wallace, Karen. *Born to be a Butterfly.* New York: Dorling Kindersley Publishing, 2000.

On the Web

FactHound offers a safe, fun way to find Web sites related to this book. All of the sites on FactHound have been researched by our staff. *www.facthound.com*

1. Visit the FactHound home page.
2. Enter a search word related to this book, or type in this special code: 1404806555.
3. Click the FETCH IT button.

Your trusty FactHound will fetch the best Web sites for you!

Index

Look for all the books in this series: